Wings of Inspiration

Robert L. Martin

ACKNOWLEDGMENTS

I'd like to thank my daughter, Renata, for her artistic and technical support during this project; she designed the cover and interior artwork, and her savvy computer skills made the rest of the job much easier. My good friend Carl DiBenedetto also helped me submit my work to the editor and figure out the ins and outs of the technology. Among the many wonderful writers on Poeticous who inspired me to keep writing, I'd like to thank Nelson D. Reyes, J Ann Crowder, C.R. Stranger, and Cory Garcia for their support throughout the years. Lastly, I want to thank my friend Linda for a lesson in brevity.

PREFACE

If someone were to ask me, "At which university did you study poetry?" I would say, "I didn't study it. I don't even know what poetry is. I don't even know who wrote it other than Khalil Gibran and Pablo Neruda."

Someone who I don't even know gives the words to me through my deepest meditations. I hear voices from somewhere. They come to me in the music I'm listening to. I believe the voices are a gift from God, and I'd better make the best of it. I will make every effort to live up to his expectations of me.

I absolutely adore poetry and music. When something moves me and makes me come alive inside, it's like something took me to some exotic paradise and filled me full of love.

My day starts out with a routine meditation in the morning about seven o'clock. I listen to Igor Stravinsky's "The Rite of Spring" to get my blood pumping. I love the wildness of the tympanis and the dissonant chordal structures in the harmony. To me, the thrill is in the dissonance; I call it melodious violence, my cathartic thrill. This is an audio violence that causes no harm, but instead moves me, moves through me, raises me; hence, my "Wings of Inspiration."

Violence makes me break the rules of poetry, which I don't even know exist anyway...and I don't care if I break them. Poetry to me is a freedom that allows me to run with the flow of the music with the words that were given to me regardless of how I'm supposed to run with them. Now, I invite you to run free with me.

CONTENTS

Aerial Slaves

Clouds of supple forming,
slaves of the whimsical winds,
moldings of the hot and cold,
sculptors of the unsettled skies,
the cathartic rants of the tempest,
the artistic lines in its face,
the lazy drifting of the stillness,
the soothing of the
sweaty palms,
obedient to the many moods,
children of the busy air,
playing beneath the
outskirts of heaven
on sacred playgrounds,
molded by the celestial breath
of the tyrannical sky master,
the aerial streams of the seasons
flowing beneath the outer spaces,
slaves of a higher authority,
obedient to their commands,
slaves of the slaves of the slaves,

the mythical tyrants,
the magic wands,
the stillness enthralled,
the sound of silence,
the music of the spheres,
the deep heavens,
the imaginary life,

the intimacy
with the living,
the traveling on and on
and on and on………

Breathing Meadows

Winter's reign in all its glory,
conquistador of the
northern skies,
overseer of the Snow Gods,
sultan of the submissive clouds,
prodding them with
sharpened spears,
breathing life into their
passive spirit,
firing lightning bolts
at their caves,
sending thunder to their doors,
releasing the snow
from their arsenals,
wreaking havoc
upon the meadows below,
choking the air supply
beneath the ground,
shaking hands with the devil,
tightening its grip upon
the face of the earth,

loosening its grip as the cold
starts its gradual dying out,
the beast of the skies
growing soft,
a requiem to its final breath,
an opening up of the air supply,
a space reserved for life to enter

and death to leave,
the breathing of the meadows
through its regenerated lungs;

an ode to life
and its coming again.

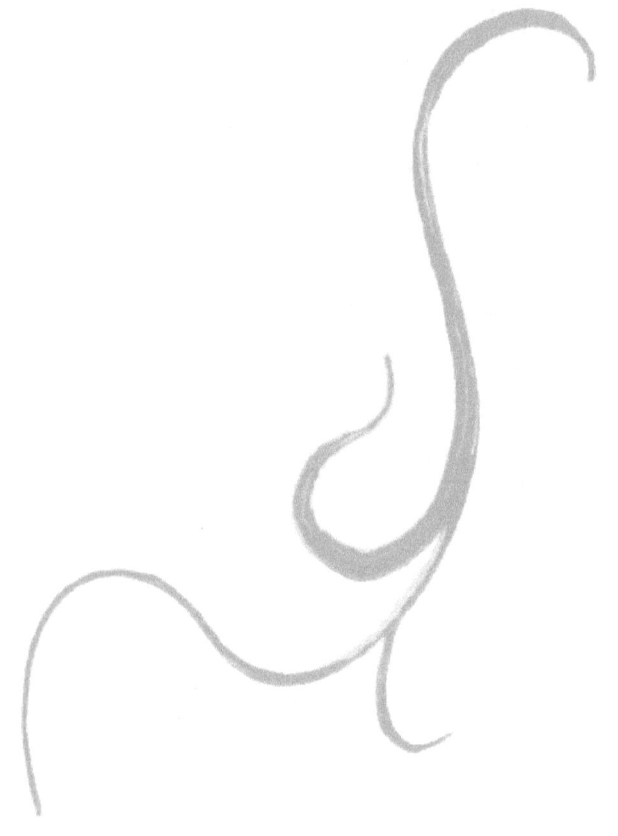

Cave Man Equipment

No cave man can do without these:
1 - a strong piece of wood for a
      handle to make a club,
2 - a big rock to tie to it for the hunt,
3 - an AK 47 assault rifle in case
      he misses the target,
4 - an open area to send smoke signals,
5 - an animal skin to fan the smoke,
6 - an Apple iphone SE 2/ smart phone
      in case someone didn't
       get the message,
7 - a hammer stone to carve a tree branch
       to make a spear to go to war,
8 - a flint arrowhead to attach to the end
       with a sharp point for a weapon,
9 - an M20A1B1 Super Bazooka in case
      the enemy didn't go down,
10 - an open area outside the cave
       to roast a pig,
11 - a cylindrical pole supported by rocks
       to hang over the fire to do the roasting,
12 - if it takes too long to cook, a 30"
       stainless steel dual fuel electric range,
13 - strong legs for the running to
       other villages to hear the news,
14 - or an ox to pull the cart to ride upon,
15 - or a new Sharp Aquos LC-30HV2U
       state of the art T.V. set
       to get the news faster.

16 - If none of the above items
serve the purpose, nothing will.
Good luck, cave man.

Chocolate

Come, thou Romeo of the salted earth,
Of mile high plateaus and steamy caves,
Of screaming palates and weakened knees,
Of bending statures and weeping pines.

I am a bride upon our eager wedding bed
With my chocolate thighs open for us,
With our tongues sweeping over our lips,
Savoring the sweetness that comes to be.

Our palates recite love poems of yore
That draw us into the maze of love and lust,
The ultimate seduction that won't let go,
That squeeze us while we bleed the sonnets.

Chocolate and lust are lovers and saints
That take us to the fire and scorch or hearts.
We speed into the blaze and lose ourselves,
Wandering toward love's sacred feast.

Chocolate and sex live in our nervous hearts,
Wrapping their tails around our minds,
Leading us to their lairs along velvet paths,
Blowing warm air into our bewildered ears.

M-m-m sweet chocolate, you naughty seductress,
You Siren on the seas, you succulent beast,
You juicy pleasure, you paradise of sex,
You den of iniquity, you enchanting witch,

You stunning sunset, you enthralling poem,
You Salome of yore, you mortal statue,
Keep me in your custody
And let me devour you
As you have devoured me.

Close to the Sound

Close to the sound
I long to be
where I can touch
and feel the
music's pulse
with my ears fastened
to its outer walls,
my heart pleading
to run inside
and make it a part of me,
to feel it melting inside me,
to feel its supple texture,
to hear it breathing,
its lungs expanding
to the corners of the earth,
its gentle waves rolling,
speaking in boisterous
and gentle tones,
its spirit engulfing me,
telling me to set myself free,
commanding me to dance,
sending thrills to my spine,
my feet, my skin, my loins,
speaking in tomes
the secret language of the spirit
melted down into celestial sighs,
pulses of the winds of paradise
wrapping around my torso,
daughters of the Gods

singing in my ears,
taking me to the deep fields
beyond the face of the Nebula,
through its harmonic doors,
up and up and up and up......
to wherever its wings
carry me to.

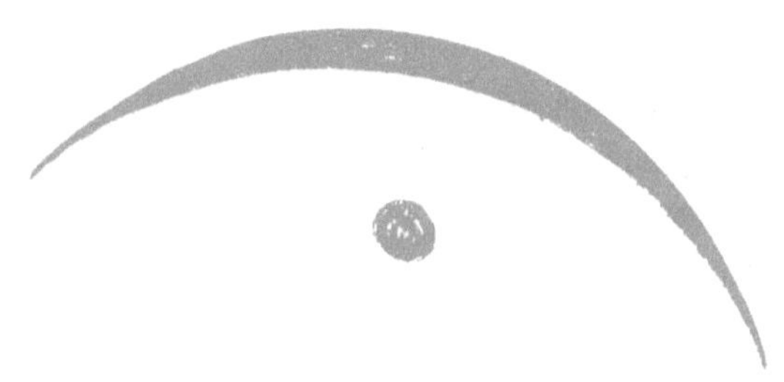

Copper Sun

Copper sun sitting
in the eastern skies
upon its fiery chariot
with a team of spirited horses
prancing and dancing
and chomping at the bit,
parting the thick clouds with
its stalwart colossal hands,
peaking out into
the waning night,
surveying its ensuing trek
across the untested firmament,
flexing its muscles
and singing the hymn
of the warriors,
lighting up its torches,
stepping out into the
forbidding rough,
the land of the
nocturnal specters,
the hands that
reach out from the graves
and snatch up
everything in its path
and take them down
into the cold earth.

"Be brave copper sun.
Be prepared. Be sure.
God be with you
on your journey."

Cyborg Priests

Victims of the internet,
the second hand voice,
the gatherers of the data,
the manufactured couriers,
the thinkers outside the online,
the thinkers inside the computer,
the gigabyte counters,
the gurus of cyberspace,
the priests of the electronic air,
the men of the new age,
the expert readers,
the collectors of the sage,
the Bible masters,
the mechanical geniuses,
the savvy button pushers,
the keyboard runners,
the finger slaves,
the dexterous utilitarians,
the simultaneous applicators,
the faster than sound movers,
the keepers of the data,

the man with the cyber spirit,
the counterfeit tear collector,
the outside man inside him,
the home of the cyber Bible,
the warehouse of the data,
the warehouse inside his mind,
the verses ingrained inside him,

the passion inside the pages,
the passion outside of him,
the disconnection of the spirit,
the loneliness of the feeling
and the desire to return again
to the priest without the
cyber Bible locked up inside.

Death Wish

A whore with no other name such is she,
tied to a whipping post to get up and flee,

a life of sadness so her story goes,
driven to see how the bad blood flows,

a slicing neat and clean upon her wrists,
a confrontation with an angel tryst,

or a sacrament at the devil's table due,
the rite of the whore, the cunning shrew,

death, a lovely rapture up ahead,
with roses piled upon her bed,

traveling to places here and far,
 midnight rides in a blackened garb,

floating through space and timeless time,
air of silence with nothing on her mind,

an empty soul in search of a better place,
with hope and finality written on her face,

her arrival at the door of the promised one,
the father she didn't know or never cared.

Demonic Engines

In underground temples with iron windows,
from under the earth in darkened holes,

engines roll with unsainted hymns
and the world's at risk as the devil grins,

pouring venom through untainted pipes,
all in the doings of the unholy rites.

The wind blows and the wicked scheme,
churning out oils and venom unseen.

couriers lined up to deliver the goods
dressed in capes with priestly hoods.

Priests dressed in robes in black and red silk,
drunk from the wine from the she devil's milk,

plow into virgins like savages at the gate
from their wicked minds in a drunken state.

Wayward pistons crank on through the night
as the engines roar 'til the dawning of the light.

As the venom leaks out into the pure air,
the sky turns red and the evil spirits glare.

It rides with the wind to faraway places
in the heat of the sun as the fire blazes.

Hell is unleashed as it sets down upon the land
and summons the Reaper to sit upon the sand,

to blow the devil's dust onto everyone and all
and comply with the works of the devil's law.

Demons In The Sanctuary

Deep down where in our sanctuary lies,
Houses of comfort and houses of longing.
Where comfort is four walls of sainted paper,
And longings are windows to look outside,
Feeling pleasure in the viewing,
Letting it fill the heart and stir the loins,
Letting it speak to the demons within,
Taking their wives to bed,
And playing with their children,
And letting love shed its morals,
And send us hither,
We let lust be the guide henceforth.
Who doesn't have these secret subdued desires?

The extraordinary are saints with no longings,
Made of steel walls and no windows,
No demons to admire outside,
No lustful pleasure to dream about,
Where love is an undefiled path to heaven
And not associated with pleasure,
That demon of the outside world.

Who is comfortable in their sanctuary?
Who is free of sin and the longing of sin?
Who can't feel lust when sex unveils itself?
Who forgoes pleasure for morality?
Who can condition himself to defy instinct?
Who can keep impure thoughts away?
Who can live in a world of bliss

And disassociate himself with the
Earthly world and earthly sensations?
Who has no demons living in his sanctuary?

Dulcis Concentus

Dulcis Concentus,
such sweet harmony,
how it selected me
from the multitudes
and flew down to me,
riding upon feathered wings
and alit upon my palate,
blowing its breath into my lungs
with a sweetness that engulfed me
and brought me to the
 gardens of Eden,
took me out into
the fields of the jasmine,
stood by and comforted me
with satiny violins
with melodious strings
moving the sound
through the romantic air,
initiated by succulent fingers
dipped in honey and spice,
harmonies that grabbed
a hold of me with its aroma
that moved through me
like a scented river
of a heavenly perfume
and threw me into the calm,
paralyzed me and
transported me through space
where I couldn't feel

anything but the sound
as it filled my lungs
and lifted me up to heaven's gate,

of such a beautiful sound,
a sound that melts all other sound,
of angel choirs and outer space,
of floating and drifting clouds,
of quiet skies and mystic rivers,
oh such sweet harmony,
Dulcis Concentus.

Elysian Preludes

Something beautiful,
something grand
of an iridescent image,
rose colored morns
drifting through
turquoise colored nights,
fiery skyborne poets
suspended in space,
rousing from a deep sleep
in coals beneath their feet,
penning the skies with
fire in their eyes,
melodies in their souls,
ballades in their hearts,
writing love sonnets,
drifting in seas of sadness,
of inspiration, strength,
drinking in the splendor
of the clouds,
building beauty in the shapes,
caressing them with their hands,
their soft fingers
running along the surface,
making music in their colors,
announcing the forthcoming
mood of the moody skies,
the playground of the clouds,
the path of the winds,

the beauty of their seclusion,
the poetry in their movement,
a divine inspiration
in the eyes of the beholder,
a harbinger of peace
born from the night
and brought out into the day,
a prelude to
an elysian meditation.

Euphonic Dawn

At the swinging open
of the curtains
that keep the phantoms
of the night away
and lets in the rays of
the living sun
at the dawning of the day,
I peered through the
cordial windows
to see the stage of
nature's theatrics,
the first act when she yawns
with the inundation of the sun,
then stretches to
soothe her rusty muscles,

then the music of the birds,
their euphonic speaking
in a language unknown that
sounds like giggling piccolos
at play high in the maples,
chatting amongst themselves
swinging from branch to branch
in a happy-go-lucky mood,
singing along with the wind
that whistles among the leaves,
and lets me know it's
time to get up
and start my daily routine.

I owe my happy mood that
gets me through the hectic day,
to the euphonic way
that I'm woken up at dawn,
by the music of the birds.

Father Nature

Connected to the rage inside
that is there and ever shall be,
the force that drives
mankind to madness from
the consuming fire from the
furnace of anger and lust
that extinguishes only before
the gratification of desire,
that anti-god born in the dark
that grows in the groin
and preys upon mother's nature,
her vulnerability and kindness,
who feels the fury of his pistons
digging holes in her sweetness,
lapping up her milk
and then running away
to set sights on the next victim,

Mother Nature of love and charity,
heroines of the fragile earth
living in the arms of God,
smiling like he does,
inhaling the pure air
and exhaling the air
made purer through her,
with the power to tame the beast,
her weakness against his strength,
her beauty against his ugliness,
her cunningness against his ignorance,

her warmth against his coldness,
breathing love into his heart,
her power over his weakness,
channeling his lust toward her only,
and molding him into a man,

Father Nature with some of
Mother Nature inside him.

Father Redwood

With thy head piercing through the skies
Reserved for the noble and for the wise
Your parlay with our God I so presume
With pen in hand in a hallowed room

Books cannot tell what you have heard
 Like a secret melody from songs of a bird
We gather together for your infinite lore
Of why love keeps coming back for more

You stand so high amongst your brothers
Is it pride that lifts you above the others?
Or your roots that grow forever and ever?
Pushing you skyward, a pilgrimage to endeavor?

We assemble together upon thy holy ground
Awed by the bright new life that we found
With love pouring through your sacred leaves
And thy mighty word sewn upon our sleeves

Father Redwood, thou art of noble heritage
Endowed with the lore of a wise old sage
Rising from a tiny seed through the years
Passing through centuries under sacred tears
Thy sermons are but a meditation in silence
But silence is enough for total reverence
Father Redwood, thank you for what you are

Fortissimo Pounding

Oceans swell and music oscillates
as nature rhymes in the rolling.
Glassy waters sit atop the motion
as eternal engines pump the seas.
Dolphins play in their quiet playground
as the fair wind blows supple kisses.
Violins murmur a soft lullaby
as the music lounges on pillows.
Tympanis fall fast asleep
as the lazy day drifts on and on.

The still winds begin their stirring
as the tempest begins to yawn.
Violins open their eyes and look around
as the wind turns up the volume.
The lazy waters get off their soft pillows
as the winds start shouting in their ears.
The horns climb on the highest wave
to sound the arrival of the tempest.

Tympanis jump out of their skin
as the tempest shakes their mallets.
Cymbals bring out the lightning
as the clashing riles up the clouds.
Piccolos start screaming
as the waves start their churning.
The murmuring seas start yelling
as the volume swells to a fortissimo.
The waves start climbing to the sky

as the engines push them high and higher.
The guts of the orchestra spill out
as the intensity pushes them back in.
The road to the climax is paved with thorns
as the waves bite into the fragile nerves.
The Gods of sound go back into hiding
as the volume increases
to a deafening fortissimo
as the universe explodes
into a million pieces,
and the madness spawns
the impending Apocalypse.

Gray Upon the Gray

Gray piled upon the restless gray
In yonder skies before me eyes,
Of beauty swirling round and round,
Ominous clouds from waters on up,
Spiraling up to the nervous skies of ebony,
Poking holes in the outskirts of heaven,
Pacing around the perimeters in haste,
Cursing at the quiet Gods inside,
Flexing their muscles and pounding their fists,
'Tis a sight to behold to see nature's rage
And beauty that grows from the deep inside.

Oh what a grand sight to approach for me,
To see Mother Nature dressed in black satin,
To take to the waters upon the crystal blue,
To paddle to see such a glorious sight
And to touch the beauty with me hands.

Into the quiet waters I go to my sightings
As beauty dances before me very eyes.
Out there in the wilds in water's rising
And me in the middle of it all.
My heart pumping outside my chest,
The waters getting wild and angry,
The waves dashing against me boat,
A ride to end all rides before,
Throwing me from one wave to another,
A thrill running down my spine,

Until that monster that put me under,
Under the deep to my watery grave,

What a price to pay;
To feel Mother Nature
Going to war
With the devil.

Gypsy Melody

Gypsies wander and melodies roam
To unfamiliar spaces to call home

Never resting, never sitting down
With their feet up off the ground

Taking flight with symphonic wings
Out in deep fields while the heaven sings

An endless journey into endless time
A haunting prelude to an easy climb

Gypsies wander with melodies and riffs
Blazing new paths among rocky cliffs

Up to the summit to the gates of the wild
And the lion's roar as nature's child

The home of the brave
with no home at all
The music keeps roaming
until the midnights fall.

Harmonie Paradis

Harmonic Paradise, my love, my heaven, my home,
my pulse, my love, my exotica, my nectar.
You await me with thy loving arms,
thy sweet breath that fills my empty chasms,
my home within a sea without a name,
my mysterious hunger that searches for a sound,
 an echo from a land behind the mist,
a palpitating language of the Gods,
a barcarole in cadence
with the motion of the tides,
a language in search of a port,
a hand unseen but a hand persuasive,
that lures me into the wilderness,
strips me naked and anoints me with exotic oils,
that casts me into a dream and stirs my passion,
a river that runs up and down my spine,
that evades my mind but finds my heart,
that music that knows me, but I don't know it,
that gets into my spirit
and transports me into a dream,
that knows how to bring tears to my eyes,
how to take over my vulnerable being,
my oblivious self that I don't know,
my rhythm that blends with thy rhythm,
my harmony that blends with thy harmony,
that sound that lives in my spirit
that responds to the sound of thy voice
of unknown origins and places and names,
that chose me among others from my world,

to overpower me with thy invisible arms,
cast me into thy seas that are a part of me,
and bring me to my home that is your home.

An ode to the power of a sound,
a sound without a name,
that came to me unheralded.

Iron Air

Higher up than the
gangly Sunflowers
that oversee the
well-being of the roses,
up higher than the top
of the white picket fence,
o'er the roof tops, the rocky cliffs;
we look up higher toward the
floor of the fat lazy cloud,
somewhere in the nigh
where wars are raged
over disputed boundaries marked
out by barbed wire fences,
where the cold iron air
battles the warm,
fighting for dominance
over the other, the eternal clash
between armies of the hot and cold,
war horses galloping in the wind,
warriors with war clubs and spears,
grenades and missiles and bombs,
louder than the loudest
clap of thunder that maims
the brittle ears of the earth
and awakens the lazy clouds
that lay around the mountain
peaks, from a deep sleep,

a war-zone below the heavens,
the tyrannical ruler of the winds,
a cold spirit rising up from the dust,
a smoldering corpse laying at its feet,
a headless specter clasping a scroll
with the secrets of the mystic skies,
the skies unseen with the naked eye,
a space beneath a deeper space,
where eternal wars are waged
as the iron air fights for dominance
in the unsettled skies,
the mightiest over the weaker.

Lab Rat

You in your voluntary innocence,
with eyes of fear, sorrow, fright,
of pain invoked from your wounds,
not knowing the whys of torture,
living in the shadows of Auschwitz,
locked up in your prison
with no room to breathe the pure air,
for a sin not in your keeping
or a crime not committed,
are the unsung hero of the world.

Your tombstone among the
rest of the fallen heroes
will have a marble plaque
upon it etched in gold
with these words that read;
"Thy service to humanity
for your heroic deeds
shall not go unnoticed."
You saved the world
from a deadly pandemic.

But you cannot read it.
If you were alive,
you still couldn't.
If you could understand
why humanity lauds you,
you couldn't.
If gold and silver were

given to you in your honor,
you would try to eat it.
If you had a brain,
you could be moved
by your accomplishments,
but then how would you have
endured all the pain inflicted
during your lowly days
in the laboratory?

Lore of the Gardens

Gardens of ancient years,
of seasonal endurance,
of high intelligence
and low mentality,
of humble charity
and proud obstinacy,
slaves of the sun and rain,
subjected to the elements,
bending under their authority,
breaking under their rage,
rejuvenated from the
flight of the pollen,
the riding with the
convalescent winds,
the sweet breath of life,
propagators of the fruits,
the restoration of the gardens,
the lore of life and
life's longing for itself.

Beautiful flowers in their
eternal botanical palaces,
the handiwork of Mother Nature,
their never changing shapes,
flaunting their proud beauty,
shimmering in the rays of the sun,
dancing with the summer breeze,
swirling their delicate skirts,
scattering a fragrance into the air,

blowing kisses to the beholders,
showing that beauty is conceited,
sensual, exhilarating to the eyes,
soothing to the heart,
and medicinal to the spirit.
'Tis the lore of the
flowers in full bloom.

Lovely Air

Currents of red and freshly green
Streams of stardust and stately clean

Moving outward from vibrant billows
Lovely air passing through the willows

Trumpets converting sound into color
Into purple haze and skies of lavender

Passion streaming from melodious winds
As the cold dies out and the music begins

Wistful melodies brought on by the sadness
Of the love of music of beauty caressed

Virgin rains and harmony in tears
Sound united in fragile ears

Passing through corridors lined in gold
Spiraling to the skies as the clouds unroll

Sound into beauty and beauty into space
Passion in control and written on the face

As trumpeters play and the music flows
Heaven drops down as the tension grows

An ode to the sweetness of the purest heart
As passion filters through from the very start

And sound turns to color as the music plays
A song of lovely air and soft summer days

Lovely Rain

Out of the sky such beauty falls
Into iridescent drops and teary balls

Through misty corridors and shiny gates
Kingly promenades and narrow straits

From natal clouds where angels cry
As spirits roam and eagles fly

Turning liquid into magic potions
Murmuring brooks into giant oceans

Lovely rain from secret hideaways
Coming into view as the sky land sways

Through hell and saintly travels so it moves
Past devil's doors and cathartic grooves

Into the mystery of the mystic dark
Into the maze of the bewildered heart

Oh such beauty as the falling rain
From a crying angel without a name

Me the Self

Me the self, my precious self,
of blood and flesh and wit,
perfect creation of man,
the treasure of treasures,
fighting for my preservation,
walking on sturdy legs
with no crutches,
standing alone
on my selfish island
in pursuit of excellence;
no helping hands, no counsel,
just me and my solitary thoughts,
my egocentric desires,

fighting for survival in a crisis
on my selfish island
with half a mind on charity,
half a mind on self preservation,
the Godly mind, the charitable one,
the guilty mind, the selfish one,
the reassessment of my goals,
the wrestling with ideals,
the climbing up the mountain or not,
the Godly, taking humanity with me,
or the selfish, leaving them behind.

Before the annihilation of humanity,
who values someone else

more than he himself?
Who values someone as much?
Who is Jesus in the heart and soul?
What is the me standing alone
on my selfish island?

He who has abundance
in himself to give,
still has enough
in himself to keep.

Mortal Glamour

Come ye see the white wings of death
See them converging at the final breath
Snow white lambs come flocking to the door
The spectacle of death and bloodshed galore

Mortal glamour so resplendent you appear
While contorted faces find death so near
Adrenalin flows with the tides of pain
With nothing to lose and nothing to gain

Snow white lambs so innocent and pure
Mouths soaked in blood their Soup Du Jour
Come off their holy seats and lose themselves
Into darkened alleys where danger dwells
Dancing with angels and demons
The dreams of the pure and white

Muse on the Loose

Thalia, Euterpe, and Terpsishore,
three naughty mythical muses,
conspiring at liberty,
having fun with my mind,
making me dance at funerals,
laugh during solemn prayers,
whistle in the
passion of the sermon,
dance during the National Anthem,
sing in movie theaters,
disrupt all solemn moods
with mocking gestures,

leaving me alone at my desk
of poetic wood constructed,
my inspirational habitat,
my utopian sanctuary,
the home that lives in my heart,
the landing platform
for all muses for the moment
at the height of my dependency,
my reliance upon their assistance,

flying around in my frustration,
laughing at my stupidity,
flitting about above my mind,
flapping their polka-dot wings,
clowns of the serious skies

on an inspirational caper,
teasing me with their whimsical minds.

Damn you, you pompous muses.
Come down from your high places.
Have mercy for my incompetence.
Come into my home, my desk.
Spill your juices into my heart.
Fill my mind with your words
you damn muses on the loose,
clowns of the sagacious skies,
mockers of everything vital,
Come down to me.

Music Tiers

One tier alone in the night,
an empty heart and empty cry,
a soloed walk in the romantic air,
a music without the sweetness,
without tiers piling up in layers,
with nothing to keep the music warm,

a frosty breath suspended in the air,
a tier alone in an empty shell,
crying through the lonely night
with arms extended but not fulfilled,
nothing to touch or embrace,
a love at the mercy of a love,
a melody at the mercy of a melody,
a something to enrich the feeling,
a piling up of beauty upon beauty,
a harmony of many colors,
of many tiers blending,
a potpourri of sound and sweetness,
a thickness prepared to travel,
a further cleansing of the clean air,
sturdy wings to keep it aloft,
a firm hand to pull it
through the fragile night,
carefully and tenderly and softly
with an assuredness not to let it fall,

a reaching into the heart
in a harmonic manner

in tiers of beauty and more beauty,
a riding upon the electric spine,
tiers invoking tears,
waters of the depths of the music,
of love invoking love,
of feeling the pulse
and hearing it breathe
through layers of many tiers.

Nocturnal Residue

The battle of the earth and sky
after the falling of the heavy sun,
the sinking under the cold horizon,
wandering along dark places,
leaving the earth exposed to
the cold, cold breath of night
that travels with the
winds of the boreal,
claiming their place in the air,
the battlefield of
the hot and cold,
the stage of
the translucent bodies
sweating in the heat of combat,
the moisture from their brows
dripping upon the grasses
before the cold air raises
its banners in victory,

until the revival of the defeated,
the reaching down for everything
that's left in its arsenal,
the lighting of their torches,
bringing up the dawn,
the rising into the purple sky,
the mounting up on their steeds,
the riding across the firmament,
drying out the nocturnal residue,

the sweat of the combatants,
the dew of the disconcerted air,
and the raising of
their banners in victory.

Oceanic Perspectives

With my feet dangling
above the clouds,
my eyes fastened to their languor,
their silky wings,
their lazy drifting along,
their parting to let the sun in
and for me to gaze
upon the oceans,
I see those dazzling blue and white
patches on the skin of the earth,
far down
beneath the clouds.

As I get off my floating perch,
anxious to get closer to them
and feel their texture
against my face,
I start falling and watch
them grow larger
enchanted by their movement,
their slow rhythmic grace.
As I get closer, the air is
filled with a briny aroma.
I can feel the texture,
the moisture of the waves.
As I dive down beneath them
with my curiosity leading me,
I can see the pulse of the waves,
their eternal perpetual engines,

the heart of Neptune throbbing,
the epicenter of activity,
the Oceanus, the mother of all
feeding her nautical children,
her rivers, streams, and lakes.
After all that, I only saw
a fragment of the workings
of our planet called earth.

Ode to Chocolate Pigs

Of service you are to mankind preferred,
to the breakfast table and also dessert,
bacon and chocolate for the appetite,
for those so addicted to such a delight.

Your alluring qualities, a magnetic force,
enticing, overpowering and open doors,
an Aphrodite you are to the common man
of flavor and charm since time began.

Chocolate pigs, when-as thy time expires,
you are taste bud heaven to such desires.
Your service to all shan't go un-noticed.
You are the flavor of heaven's kiss.

Outside Poemland

Outside Poemland
where the air is cold,
the trees are trees and
the words are words.

Inside Poemland
where the air is warm,
trees are the fruits
of the Botanical Gods,
cast down to earth
as sentries to guard
the meadows and
adorn the hills.

Words are words
painted in dazzling colors,
flowing out of the heart,
taking to the sky and
skirting around the facts,
not quite landing,
but teasing the intellect
into thinking that
they have to land
even though they won't.

Take me to Poemland
and let me ride
with the words.

Perimeters

In the wake of the storm
after the tempestuous beatings
upon the face of the earth,
when the end seemed like a
mythical dream, a fairy tale,
a far off ecstasy in another time,
behold the weariness of the storm
from its domination over
the fragile skies,
the weakening of its power,
its looking behind to see
what it left hanging in the azure skies,
the adornment of the naked firmament,
the rainbows in their full glory,
a readying for the gala of the skies,
the festivities of the celestial spirits,
the images of their
moving into the eyes
and hearts of the beholder
and putting stories
and fantasies in their minds.

When I fly to the skies
I want to see the perimeter
of the rainbow,
to feel the texture,
the softness of its body,
to go inside and feel the colors
and see what they do to my skin,

how they send a thrill to me,
how they ride up and down my spine,
how the aroma fills my lungs
and lifts me up closer to heaven
my new home, my new paradise,
my new spirit, my new me,
drifting in and out of the perimeters.

Poseidon's Song

Song of the fury
While tempests chant
Gnawing at the nerves
Like evil dogs
The beauty of the skies
Layers upon layers of
Glistening black arms
Dancing to the
Rites of the macabre
Thunder clapping
 Tympanums clamoring
Half beauty, half terror
Half passion, half deadly
Beautiful danger moving ahead
With loaded arsenals singing
Flirting with romance and death
Angry barcaroles
Composed by Davy Jones
 Hymns of glory to sinking bodies
Of ships in their fateful descending
Landing on blackened floors
Phantoms away from sunlit waters
Falling into cold dark tombs
Into the cradle of Hades
Poseidon's Song to the
Fate of the sailor
Sailing on stormy seas

Power And Power

Surging tempest and heaving waves
Swirling winds and seafarers' graves

Angry volcanoes with contorted faces
Spitting fire thru' iron clad cases

Catching the wind and throwing it back
Scattering the thunder in skies so black

Pushing the earth all around the sun
As easy as the spider's web tightly spun

Eternal power, an engine that won't quit
That can rise and command the stars to sit

Or the power that pushes the roses up thru'
As life gives to life and obligations hold true

The power that hushes the murmuring brooks
With mandates written from the ancient books

The power that touches the tender heart
That loosens the tears and cries as they part

The eternal power that brings lovers to lovers
Giving them its blessing as heaven hovers

Power, how thou art so mighty and tender
Giving to the earth and stars in splendor

Working thy magic and never falling down
Stay as you are, so secure and tightly bound
Reigning over the universe thou kingly crowned

Prelude to a Waterfall

Silent waters with mobile desires,
beset with a nomadic spirit,
trapped inside the river banks,
buried in ancient catacombs,
prisoners of the quiet earth,
serving out their
temporary incarceration
with a mind to break away
and run with the rain,
to dance through the rocks
and swim to the
ends of the earth,

to be moved by
the tears of the clouds,
the liberators of the spirit,
the heroine of the skies
who oversee the
solemn faces of the still water
with their dreams
of running and dancing
and laughing and
flowing with the current.

Alas the gentle drifting,
the stirring of the stillness,
the following along
the river banks,
picking up the pace

with the undulating earth,
the union with the other waters
with the ends of the earth in sight,
the cascading down rocky cliffs,
the release of the nomadic spirit
in columns of the white waters,
the racing with a joyful heart,
the breaking out of prison,
the singing of freedom songs,
the coming to the ends of the earth
and the witnessing of the falling waters.

Random Dispersals

Beneath the inferno pits,
the hell hole in the unfathomable,
the seed of evil germinating
in unholy gardens,
an imminent breaking through
the rancid fertile soil,
a nurturing by the blackened sun
and the reddened rain,
a falling of the blood of the angels,
a rising of the devil's fruit,
emergent apocalyptic weapons
breaking out of their iron shells,
a poison looking for another poison,
an Adam looking for an Eve,
a devil looking for another devil,
looking for its propagation
and a random dispersal
of an unseen poison,
the devil's spume
flying through the air
looking for a lonely host,
to dive down into his sweet lungs,
then be transmitted to
another lonely host
until humanity is down
on its knees
and the world
is at the devil's feet.

Raptus Adhesion

Nature's unseen hands of sorcery
in the throes of beauty unguarded
and beauty exploited,
reaching down into
the arena of desire,
deep down into the heated groin,
the epicenter of a rapacious motion
in response to nature's calling,
drawn to its adhesive scent
where there's no turning back,
to breathe in the perfume
of the wild jasmine and run with
the pulse of the wild drums,
flowing into the heated ochre rivers,
down to the valley
of the sainted wolves,
to feast with the lions
and dance to the rite of passion
and take in the rapture
from the call of beauty,
its tender kisses on the skin,
its touch on the electric spine,
its seductive commands in the ear
to run through the fires
into the heat of demonic dreams
and climb the mountain with them,
and stand atop the summit
and breathe in the sweetness of the air
from the magic powers

of nature's hands
that keep me in its grasp,
that raptured feeling,
that raptus adhesion,
until the last
breath is released
into the sweet, sweet air.

Ripple

Sill water in a glassy state,
a child of the immobile air,
reflecting the beauty
of the surrounding elements,
luxuriating in the early morn,
a lazy lake with no dreams,
no where to go, nothing to do,
vulnerable to a falling leaf,
to a drop of rain,
the breeze, the wind, the storm,
the temper of the clouds,
the sultan of the lower skies,

the coming of a forceful entry,
the alarm of an outside stimulant,
a wind blown acorn from a tree,
a force to distort the
smoothness of the surface,
to disfigure the mirrored beauty
of the surrounding elements,
the nervousness of the
agitated waters,
a ripple that became a
ring of ripples,
a gradual expanding from the center,
a growing of the heights,
the transformation
of a ripple to a wave,
a reaching up into the air

to meet the wind and rain,
a dashing to the shoreline,
a beating against its banks,
then a waiting out
for the storm to clear,
then a dying down to a ripple,
then the lazy smoothness,
then the mirrored elements again,
then back to the beauty of the lake.

Scribal Slaves

I of service to the poet Gods,
the kinds with no hands nor feet,
but keen eyes, celestial minds
and tyrannical tongues,
chose me, a man with no dreams,
contented with what I was,
to be their scribal slave.

They stuffed their words
into my empty mind until they
irritated the outer walls.
They commanded me
to write them down.
They hovered over my bed
and wouldn't let me sleep.
They oversaw the results
and berated me for
my incompetence.
They wouldn't leave me alone
until they were satisfied
with my work.

But their inflexible demands
took me to a higher place
where I became a
pure part of the abyss.
I saw the universe and
heard it speaking and

felt it against my face.
I became a poet.

Then they left me alone with my
inspiration drained from me.
They floated back to
where they came from;
from the alleys, the streets,
the silence, the brooks, the earth,
the sky, the clouds, the sun,
somewhere hidden from
the eyes of my mind.

Sea Of Magic

As I climbed up onto the highest mount,
Too many steps along the way to count,
I reached the gateway to loveless peak,
Where nothing grows, nothing there we seek.

Love was below where the water lies,
Where I started my climb beyond my eyes.
It called out to me in its secret tongue,
Like barcaroles of enchanted sea farers sung.

"I am love below floating in the current.
My waves are listless as heaven hath sent.
My surface shimmers in the morning light,
    And my mysterious depth runs deep into the night.

I am of poetic heritage, of language unknown.
I speak through the heart, from my furrows sown.
Love is my garden and I am the wizard of the rain.
    I live in the Sea Of Magic where lovers lay claim."

Segue into Paradise

The iron arms of tragedy,
a paradox of strength and infirmity,
builders and destroyers of character,
lodged inside the flesh and soul,
the teeth of the hidden devil
at home in his new home,
his paradise built from the ugly virus,
from his missiles that hit the target,
his mission accomplished,
his heavy stain on the human heart,
his wounds hitting the bottom
with no where else to go,
starting on an upward trend,
on a convalescent journey
with his strength leaking into the soul,
becoming fused with the good,
the Godly, the all powerful,
the devil's heedless rebuilding
in progress,
leaking into the spirit,
the epicenter of mankind,
the heartener of a new spirit,
a new strength to replace the old,
the building blocks of
the house of the future,
the paradise of the worthy ones
who earned their good fortune
from overcoming
the strength of the devil

and his unknowingly
segue to paradise,
the house of the future.

Sensations

As potters move through moistened clay
As lovers melt from skin so soft
As velvet slides through fervid fingers
And passion surges like spinning rivers

Tempos pounding like mad tympanis
To singing loins and quickened pulses
Clay is not clay, but a sensual song
Of melting steel and weeping warriors

Love so resolute, love so pliant
Pass through my fingers to my loin
Of thy tears, a presidio has been built
Within my soul, my poetic strength

Play thy song, my celestial troubadours
As your moisture slides up to heaven

I come to the potter's wheel as an
Apprentice and leave with a
Sensation that only romantic
Potters can feel

Stages of the Infinite

Knowledge is the
whole of many parts
of which one is the
beginning of the next,
which is still countless
miles away from
the whole completed.

Congratulations graduates.
You have completed
      one stage leading
up to the infinite.
What are your plans
for the next stage?
Another graduation?

That Tree of Mine

That tree of mine
Even though it isn't,
Stands outside my window
All dressed up in summer green.

If I talk to it and give it a name,
Can't I say it belongs to me?
It responds when I tell it
To shed its leaves in autumn
And get ready for the snow,
Then get rid of the snow again
For summer's warming days.
If it does all those things for me,
Why can't I say it's mine?

The Driven Winds

From sources and cryptic hideaways,
where life is an unseen force,
where it moves without arms and legs
but colossal wings and adhesive tentacles,
where aerial giants roam the busy skies
as they have been doing since time began,
singing with the angels,
playing with the clouds
or dancing with the devil,
whoever sends them along the way,
loyal disciples of all tyrannical forces,
anointing the still air or riling up the clouds,
flying with the angels or cursing at them,
a force without a mind
but an instinctive demeanor,
an object stilled by the torpid air,
waiting for its master to move it along,
to live again and play in the nimble skies,
to jump into the clouds and stir them up,
to blow them as hard as it can,
to watch the seas toss the ships around,
to marvel at the swirling waters,

or makes way for the rainbow,
the beauty in the majestic skies,
the peacemaker that upholds
the law of the earth,
the winds of peace
that speak to the trees,

the violets, the birds, the creatures,
that weep with the pain of the hunt
and the agony of the hunted,
and revels with the greening of the hills,
the new spirit that takes over the earth,
a renaissance of nature's dream,
the driven winds that kiss the earth
and romance the budding gardens.

The Hood

Of days gone by
but still clinging on,
still grasping at his sleeve,
still riding on his back,
in his mind, in his attitude,
the camaraderie of the idlers
that glues them together,
spreads throughout the hood
and stays in the hood,
stayed with him
during his escape
into a new world of
prosperity and success.

Camaraderie lingers in his heart
like a mother that lost her child.
Reminiscence brightens the spirit
when it grows dark in
the days of uncertainty.
The dark side of the nature of man
has to surface as it did before.
It is always there no matter
how much of it is covered up.
Camaraderie left its stain in his life.

His prosperous mind is discontent.
Ten million dollars earned is less
than one hundred dollars begotten.
The thrill that keeps the blood boiling

is gone during the transaction;
in the not knowing of the outcome.

This poor millionaire is a
slave of the hood mentality.
No matter how hard he tries
to leave it behind, he can't.

The Losing

The tightening of the straps,
the dam that impedes the flowing
of the river that runs
to places unknown,
the numbing of the passion,
the protocol of the common man,
the ethics and the fear of ethics,
the bindings that dig into the spirit,
the writings that control the writing,
the rules from the book of poetry,
the rhetoric of the high and mighty,
the words that categorize words,
the love that regulates love,
the heavy hand that abuses it,
the weight that falls on the free spirit,
for the demands to lose its authority,

at last the feeling of the free air,
the losing of the weight,
the pressure it has on the spirit,
on the mind, the heart, the soul,
the lifting them up and
casting them out into the abyss,
the opening up of the imagination,
the running into the wilderness,
the floating over mountain peaks,
the playing in the clouds,
running with the rivers of passion,
the freedom song of the poet,

the emancipation of the words,
the refinement of their voices,
the love of the sound they make,
and the effect they have
upon the ears of the heart,

at last the losing of the
rules of the book of poetry.

The Lotus

Water, air and sun
My Goddess I thee worship
My home, my temple

My petals, my palms
Bonded together in prayer
An ode to the sun

The air gives me breath
The water keeps me afloat
I am a Lotus

The Revival

The revival of love
once bestowed in the hearts
of the devoted,
the teachers with the seed
still growing in their being,
after years of longing
for the blossoming to
spread again in the mind,
seeking its revival
from the prisons of age,
to ride upon the wings
of knowledge and seek
its worthy recipients again,
the students of the new order
with curiosity streaming
from their absorbent minds,
ready for his wisdom to enter
and lead them to the
place they want to be;
where their dreams
told them about,

they arrive at the
gates of their desires
with the passion of his love
leading them through dark
corridors with its fiery torches,
instilling the love from
his heart into their hearts,

his faith into their faith,
his wisdom into their lives,
his understanding
into their souls
through the passion and
dedication to his
love of teaching
that lingered in his heart
throughout his idle years.

The Roots

The foot of the leg of the body
The foot under the soil of the earth
The stubborn oak tree
The entrenchment in the steadfast ground
The roots on the way to the core
The heart and guts of the earth
The iron truth of the nature of man
The immunity from any alterations
The sanctions from the Biblical Garden
The history of mankind
The birth of the beast and the lamb
The seeds of passion implanted
The loves and hates forming
The blossoming of the ego
The permanence of the self in place
The moving toward independence
But still the clinging on to
Biblical Garden sanctions
The living under their authority
The power of their influence
With a futile attempt to lose them
But the submission of the self to them
The acceptance of their inborn laws
And the resignation of the self to them

The natural resistance to anyone
who tries to change the
nature of mankind
the cerebral thinkers

the law makers
the rebels
the protesters
and the rioters
who think they
can but never will

The Scattering

Chariots of springtime in the air unseen
Blowing with the wind in quiet green

Lightly with the wind beneath their wings
Dancing in the glen as the zephyr sings

Pollen scattered throughout the heart of day
To the fruitless fields and further away

To the ends of the earth from winter's wake
Laying down as the soothing winds overtake

A settling down in fields of future's barley
Giving life with a new spirit running free

A sacred rite in the eyes of the sun
An eternal rendezvous since time begun

A landing from where the soft winds blew
A scattering of the pollen to a life anew

The Second Wave

After the calming of the
first assault comes the second
wave of the virus of the
devil's army with a vengeance
upon the shores of the thinkers,
the physicians and lab workers,
the Davies in opposition
with the Goliaths,
the slingshots with a faith
and a brain against
the muscles of the Covid beast,
the disciples of the devil
with seven empty heads.

As they reach the shores
with their spears affixed
flexing their iron muscles,
not knowing about the
secret arsenals hidden
in the interior regions
in the brains of the thinkers,
the generals and scientists,
the ones who learned from
the first assault, knowing
what to do when
the second comes,
they jump into the fire
not knowing how hot it is.

With the battle of Armageddon
still raging in their memories,
the thinkers rise up with
their formulas and vaccines,
led by courage, determination,
and a faith in God almighty,
the supreme thinker of them all,
and stand upon the hill
waving their cerebral banners
in victory over the second wave.

The Selection

From the busy skies, or bellowing streets,
or whistling winds, or forest nymphs,
or cathartic fires, or emancipated souls,
someone or something picked me out,
me among the crowded streets,
a speck hidden among the multitudes,
me a massive target, bigger than life,
to select me for what I know not,
my eyes looking at my shuffling feet,
my mind wandering into the pale blue sky,
emptied of all thought and denial,
my little self in tune with impartiality,
contented with my easy shuffling.

Then it came to me and rattled my bones,
a voice, an arrow that pierced my spine,
an epiphany that I wasn't looking for,
that blinded me and took me upon a journey.
A euphonic river flowed into my soul,
repeated verses and sonnets in my ears,
and dragged me into dark alley ways,
along stately thoroughfares,
manicured gardens, and into a lofted cathedral
where I awoke and looked around
at the new me, the me laden with heavy words,
the me with new wings to take me wherever,
and the me that I thought I would never be.

Why someone is selected is a mystery.
Poetry is a non-discriminate spirit that
looks for anyone to enter into.

The Sighting

Stumbling through the darkness
I moved with no eyes,
no arms, no ears,
just a distant memory
of objects in deep thought,
like a river looking for its origin,
running with no eyes
but a feel of the twists and turns
leading back to the source
and a silent authority
telling it to run;
that there is a light,
and all uncertainty will pass
like the seasons of
joy and sorrow
winding around each other,
like the fear of the night
running into the light of day.

Time is a messenger of hope
arriving at the shores of despair
with news of a forthcoming joy,
a sighting of a
faint glimmer of light,
a beacon pointing to
the end of the tunnel.

All viruses and disasters
have run their course.

All things have come and passed.
Time has galloped in
on its white horse and
shortened the gap between
despair and prosperity.

The Spire

On the day of the
winter solstice,
I see a tapering spire
outside my window
atop an old building
across the street,
pointing at the sunrise
in a proud stance,
telling me to look up
into the sky and find the sun
so I can be able to foresee its
leftward advancement
toward the summer solstice,
a journey that would take
six months to reach,
six months of snow to rain,
from the pangs of winter
to the joy of summer days
in its slow moving progression,
teaching me about patience,
that it will happen eventually
and my spirits will be lifted.

My revitalized feeling
will overcome
my nervous anticipation
and the joy of it will be greater
when I can feel and remember
what it was lifted from.

An ode to the
old spire, the sun,
and their
therapeutic counseling.

The Subduction of Anxiety

The tides of anxiety as if
the flowing was immobile,
as if it was a wave
glued to the sandy shore,
when time was a standstill horror,
a knife lodged in the joyful heart,
the pain of a never-ending sorrow,
a time when death was a paradise,
an easy way out of the misery,
a weight that will never be lifted,
the immobility of time
stuck in the dreaded present
never to move forward to the light,
future's heroic rescue mission,
an ebb tide rolling back to sea,
back into the calm again
with spirits on the mend
and the restoration of hope
forming in the hearts and minds.

Alas the subduing of anxiety,
of fear losing its grip,
the rolling back into the calm,
the future starting up again,
its legs gathering strength,
its eyes opening up
and seeing the path up ahead
and how it flows with the ebb tide,
the way it drifts back to the sea

with an invitation to flow with it
and not rush to get back to normal,
but in sync with its natural course,
a natural rolling
with the tides of time,
the restoration of joy
and a trust in future's evolution.

The Surfacing

The far beneath and far inside,
a million fathoms and a million miles,
the home of the abyss,
the nothing seen
but everything valued,
treasures hidden in the depths,
eternal engines kicking their feet,
birds of mystery flapping their wings,
Magus lighting up the dark,
internal secrets clawing at the walls,
the heart of the substance
pulsating at a fever pitch,
the mystery of the deep out of view,
curiosity building with each thought,
the arms of intrigue grabbing
a hold of the mind, the body,
the heart, the spirit, the soul,
the beauty inside in
a seductive mood
coming outside of its shell
with its eyes of deep oceans,
its rose gardens permeating the air,
its blood surging through the veins,
its music filled with intensity,
its many fathoms taking form,
its engines running at full capacity,
lighting up the
callous chasms of the soul
with their fiery torches,

prose running at full speed,
the pulse of the music
coming to the surface
as the many fathoms
come into view
revealing their internal secrets,
their touch with infinity,
and their travels in the divine.

The Taming

As passion runs into the wilds
with its machetes and missiles
into the fires of Gomorrah,
its heart running full speed ahead,
its brain left behind
at the academies of higher learning,
its mouth tasting the
blood of the daughters of Eros,
its wings lifting it off the ground
claiming the skies above,
the avenue to the diabolic paradise,
full steam ahead with no
thought of letting up,
resisting any kind of taming,

a beast and always a beast
alone in its lonely asylum,
a beast with a hidden heart,
a silent pumping
of an exotic blood,
a surging of the warmth
from a secluded calling,
a gradual longing for
the brain that was left behind,
a conscience dead and buried,
a desire to bring them back,
to restore that long lost
amiable feeling in the heart,
to reach out for someone

and see that someone
longing for the same thing,

the taming of the beast,
of passion unattended
leading to the curtailment
of its wild running in
compliance to its own desires.

Trumpets of Passion

Embryonic sound budding
in the melodic heart
and lovely mind,
primal voices under
the direction of divine grace,
harps of heaven,
angelic trumpets,
melted violins, crimson sunsets,
glassy seas, shooting stars
out in deep space,
nature's mystic land,
heaven's breath traveling
through the walls of time,
home of the melodic heart,
a garden of the jasmine
blowing the sweet scent
that rises into the fragile air
and rides with the zephyrs,
compiling airy thoughts,
of tuneful portrayals of heaven,
the blending of the poetic heart,
wolves of the wild and quiet lambs,
the passion and
the running of passion,
of whispered melodies
and dexterous fingers
caressing the valves, the slaves
of the trumpet,
carrying the sound to open places,

sweeter than the sound that entered,
converting the beautiful
into the extraordinary,

the trumpet and the man
and the conversion of
heavenly thoughts.
Oh sweet sound,
Oh that sweet sound.

Voices in Hiding

Up high beyond the world
of terrestrial thought,
free from linear delineations,
hidden in dreams and meditations,
a look into divine revelations,
the fluidity of poetic verse,
voices locked inside a vault,
heard by the saints with a key
but not the seeker who
opens it only through
deep meditation
when it becomes available,
but sometimes not,
sometimes it comes
from nothing at all,
a showering of words
onto random surfaces like
a rain that falls onto
an already flooded street,
or a poem that falls
onto a casual stranger
looking for a place to sit
with his mind focused
on terrestrial thoughts
with no idea what to do with it,

but for the seeker an epiphany,
a look into the loving universe,
a vision of the home of the saints,

the nocturnal sky perforated
by starry flashes and arrows,
the new dawn of a new mind,
a new rain upon a new shoulder,
a prose unheard and unexplained
from the opening of the vault,
the words from the high heaven,
from the voices in hiding
in their random falling.

Warriors of the Morn

Stallions flying
in the blackened sky,
galloping steeds, chariots ablaze,
liquid smoke of copper red,
streaming across the firmament,
battle ready giants in their glory,
battle cries with piercing voices,
perforating the night with
bloody spears, wielding swords,
biceps bulging, shredding shirts,
flaunting black aegises, fists of iron,
hands of stone, waving banners,
brandishing skulls on poles,
all in a day for the
warriors of the morn,

and warriors springing up
from their underground nests,
their regeneration stations
of lightning bolts and robotic parts,
razor talons and pterodactyl wings,
rising up in the eastern skies,
battling the clouds,
burning through the thick haze,
charging into the black smoke,
carrying the sun on their backs,
fighting fire with fire,
looking westward
to the thick of the battle,

grinding their teeth,
swallowing their hearts,
readying for the
westward journey
with the sun blazing the way,
all in a day for the
warriors of the morn.

Waterfall

Waterfall of a perilous beauty,
of pastel wings and thorns about,
angel abodes with demonic doors,
living water falling down from
deadly currents breathing life into it,
a gilded heaven revealed
from behind the misty curtains,
nature's eternal silent symphony
dancing down from jagged cliffs
in cadence with the oceans of time,
beauty in aqua green emeralds falling,
faces in the sunlight of precious gems,
artistic world moving at a furious pace,
from far off sightings, a masterpiece,
nature's unassuming work of genius,

From intimate associations, a hell,
a beast that adorns a holy mask,
where power is the supreme evil,
the touch, a falling into wicked hands,
a compliance to a sorcerer's request,
the downward journey, a deadly ride,
the smashing into the razor like rocks,
the sound of mortal laughter,
the aftermath, a mission of the devil done,

Beauty in her glory, in her aesthetic shining,
her visual grandeur, her humble greatness,
her flight in the company of angels,

her walking with the spirit of the winds,
her place in the assembly of the Gods,
her understanding of their sacred language,
her intelligence of humble origins,
brought forth in the winds of wisdom
and the love of nature and its construction,
of its ways and unassuming beauty,
of beauty in awe of beauty.

An ode to her charm
and apprehension to her peril.

Waters of the Wild

Born in the throes of Mother Nature,
from internal engines in the deep
at the mercy of the tides
and their authority,
ancient engines manufactured
by the genius of nature,
far from the eyes of the beholder
who gazes through rose colored glasses,
swooning at the artistic movement,
the rolling in from the deep,
the lines of pure white liquid velvet,
a seascape that breathes and flaunts itself,
a motion that stays with
the eyes of the heart
like musical strokes of the baton
in the hand of the orchestral conductor,
the kissing of the rocks,
the artistic movement of the splashing
like liquid angels dancing in the sun,
the tears caressing the sand,
gathering up the pebbles and
taking them back out to sea again,
a loving duty performed by
Mother Nature in her tranquil mood,

the feel of her strength up close,
to see a mountain of water looming,
arsenals hidden in its fury,
the straying from the easy,

the poetic rhythm of motion,
of ferocity in its christening,
of confusion with no place to settle in,
of the wild going out into the wild,
of mass destruction from the pounding,
tossing the ships like rag dolls,
tons of steel floating in the wind,
the devil's spume passing though
evil mouths and razor like fangs,
Mother Nature in her brutal attacks,
her passion and the
running of her passion.

Weavers of the Clay

Fatherly fathers,
potters of the clay,
ambassadors of morality
and knowledge,
inheritors of obligations,
relinquishing their
self fulfilling desires,
giving up their selfish dreams,
molding their sons and daughters
on the potter's wheel
with sagacious hands
and careful fingers,
defining and representing
moral integrity and providence,
planting seeds in their minds,
overseeing their development
while not interfering
with their decisions,
encouraging them to be
what they want to be
and not what you are.

You are only the potter
and not the pottery.

Wildflower

Wild is the flower
in meadows unsown,
far beneath the Himalayan peaks
wreathed by regal clouds,
picturesque patches of green,
moving shades of purple,
riding with the roving sun,
galleries of nature's handiwork,
hiding behind the craggy cliffs
that divert the rolling streams
from snow into ice into water
into sporadic fertile fields,
down into the porous soil,
the mother of the wild flower,
trattoria of the animals,
work place of the bees,
academy of botanical science
for the students of nature,
one single flower,
microcosmic world
drawing them to the core,
shrinking them down to
the life of a bee,
flying onto the petals,
luxuriating in the air,
drinking the nectar,
witnessing the fountain of life,
drawn to the spathe and
sensing the lust,

understanding the magnetism,
then growing back
to normal again
with a knowing of another
segment of how nature works
and taking one step closer
to finding the way
to the shadows of God.

Wings of Inspiration

Transitory wings of white and gold,
beauty in flight and rivers in motion,
doors swinging open for the pure air,
clarity speaking in a familiar tongue,
divinity opening up its heart,
sending secrets through the skies,
the birth of the planets,
the texture of the rings of Saturn,
how it feels against the skin,
writing them down and
attaching them to the wings of the doves,
circling above with their eyes wide open,
purifying the air above the chimneys,
breathing in the aroma of the jasmine,
keeping love pure on its earthly journey,
the knowledge of its divine source,
how it flows through winding rivers,
why it ends up in certain places
answering spiritual needs
or landing upon insensitive surfaces,
how it materializes in certain objects,
how it invigorates the spirit
of some but not in all,
how it gives life to a song, or poem,
or speaks through a rainbow or
the eyes of a woman,
how it teases the mind and
rides up and down the electric spine,
taking the spirit on a merry romp,

smiling, laughing, playing, crying,
riding to the ends of passion,
then flying back to that
wonderful place where it came from
too soon, too fast, too impatiently,
too abrupt, too detached,
but with its taste still in our hearts.

Yellow Harbingers

The rites of spring,
the emptying of the snow clouds
onto the pale gray meadows,
the home of the life that once was,
the funeral of the fallen leaves,
the tomb of the flowers,
the wearying of the shivering maples,
the answered prayers
of the mortal gardens,
the melting of winter's snows,
the reaching down
into the bowels of the earth,
the epicenter of activity,
the breathing of the heart of life,
deep down into the sunken gardens,
the yawning from a deep sleep,
the moving of the pliant limbs,
the rising of the anxious sprouts,
the proud standing against the sun,
the resuscitation of the
Forsythia bushes,

the stirring of the buds,
the looking out into the sun
through their yellow eyes,
a sighting beyond belief,
moving with the rites of spring,
dancing with the warming zephyrs,
repeating a song of joy

in unison with the spirit of life,
announcing the coming of the
warmth of the impending days,
the duty of the yellow harbinger
from a little Forsythia bush
out in the meadows of the wild.